SKOM
MEMO...

C000067718

With my deepest thanks to my wife Christine
for all her painstaking work in editing this story and
in asking the right questions to revive old memories.

I also share these memories with my sisters
June and Valerie who I hope will enjoy these
reminders of our many happy years growing up on
Skomer. We also shared the sadness when
we left our beloved island home for the last time.

My thanks also to the Wildlife Trust of South and
West Wales who kindly provided a rare opportunity
to rekindle vivid memories of our family's life
on Skomer during some very challenging times.

Preface

This story starts on a sunny day in 1922 when my grandmother Cecilia Sturt was in London meeting friends and indulging in a little shopping. Life was good for Cecilia and Walter Sturt, a retired dentist of some renown, and their only child Betty, who were looking forward to a relaxing retirement enjoying their new holiday home in Dawlish in Devon.

On that day in London, while Cecilia was killing time between appointments and doing a little window shopping, she came across the London office of Knight Frank & Rutley the estate agents. Idly glancing at what was currently available, as one does, she noticed that Lord Kensington in Pembrokeshire was disposing of some of his estate - four islands, together with some adjoining estate.

On little more than a whim, my grandmother decided that it would be nice to own some islands - and thus the scene was set for a life that would be so different from normal expectations. In their new Pembrokeshire home, Betty would eventually meet and fall in love with Reuben Codd, the youngest son of a local farmer, and these two young people, from such widely different backgrounds, would elope to get married.

It is at this point that we take up the story of life for the Codd family on Skomer island - a life that was delightful in so many ways, but also deeply demanding and challenging. Nature seemed to throw every impediment in their way, and it was a constant battle to overcome each challenge, but dogged determination and the sheer magic of island life gave them the strength to persevere against all the odds.

However, Reuben and Betty Codd had differing expectations from life and, after some years of trying to make island farming pay its way, it eventually became clear that this was just not possible. Moreover, as the years passed, the demands of island life were becoming ever more difficult to deal with, and my parents finally decided that there was simply no option but to sell their beloved Skomer island and go their separate ways.

In the following pages I have set out to recapture the ups and downs of island farming life, when communications were very basic and a world war intervened to make life even more challenging. - So very different from today's world.

A very special place

What is it that makes an island such a very special place? No doubt the sense of remoteness from the everyday trials and tribulations of the world outside is part of its attraction, but for many it is often much more than that. The unique mix of the geology, the wildlife, the landscape, and the human story of achievement - often in very difficult circumstances, all combine to stimulate sensations that can be utterly enthralling and captivating - a different world.

 Now imagine that you actually own that island, where that unique mix is deeply embedded in your everyday life. If you then

Looking west towards Skomer Island from the old

1

move away, a deep void is left that is never quite filled. That is how I, and my sisters June and Valerie, feel about Skomer island, where we lived during our most formative years. The almost overpowering scent of the bluebells in the Spring, the raucous clamour of thousands of sea birds during the breeding season, the seals defending their pups, and the absolute tranquillity that can descend when all of that is over - that was our much loved family home.

But that was only a part of our island life. The winter months produced a very different and more challenging backdrop to our lives. Strong and often extremely damaging gales were relatively routine during the winter months, producing mountainous seas which battered the shoreline and were a constant threat to the safety of our boats - our only lifeline with the mainland. Yet in a strange way this tough and challenging part of our island life was just as rewarding and stimulating as the calmer times.

Coastguard hut on the Deer Park at Martins Haven

The young Codd family in 1935 - the year before Valerie was born

A little bit of history

My grandfather, a retired dentist, had bought Skomer, Grassholm, Midland and Gateholm islands from Lord Kensington when his estate was broken up in the early 1920s. Gateholm sits along the coast at one end of Marloes sands, and is only an island at high tide. Midland island sits between Skomer and the mainland and has little to attract visitors, although my sisters and some friends camped there on occasion. Grassholm sits ten miles out in the Atlantic beyond Skomer, and is host to one of the largest colonies of gannets in the world.

Gannets on Grassholm don't believe in wasting space

Ubiquitous Puffins on Skomer

Guillimot on egg - on a ledge in Skomer North Haven

Skomer is by far the largest of the four islands at just under one thousand acres. It is a sea bird sanctuary of considerable note, and has been inhabited on-and-off since Neolithic times. There had been many tenant farmers of the island over the centuries, but our family were the first – and last - owners of the island to commit their lives to protecting its heritage whilst also striving to make a living from its fertile land.

Whilst its land was indeed highly fertile, and its surrounding waters rich in marine life, exploiting those advantages came at an extraordinarily high financial and personal cost. It was in the early 1930's, after their runaway marriage, that my father and mother took up the challenge of farming Skomer, and facilitating special studies of the flora and fauna that are unique to the island - such as the Skomer vole.

They were always particularly keen to welcome research studies by the University of Wales at Aberystwyth, and other naturalists who were fascinated by Skomer's unique features. One unsuccessful experiment was when a pair of Golden Eagles were brought to Skomer to see if they would settle there and breed. Skomer's craggy cliffs seemed to hold promising possibilities as a suitable terrain for these majestic birds. For a while it looked as though the gamble would pay off, until there was a particularly bad winter gale. The eagles were never seen again.

The farming challenge that Father and Mother faced was considerable. Potato crops lost their premium due to the delays implicit in picking and bringing the crop to market from a remote island. Transport of the superbly fattened livestock on Skomer's ultra-verdant vegetation also needed extra labour to be brought from the mainland to help to facilitate that difficult crossing in an open boat. The cards were always heavily stacked against commercial success.

And so it was that in 1950 my family gave up the unequal struggle. Our lovely island home was sold to Mr Leonard Lee, a West Midlands industrialist, and my father and mother divorced and went their separate ways. Both loved the island very much, but the ever constant hard grind of island life had taken its toll. Moreover, they had long had a somewhat tempestuous relationship, driven by different expectations of life, and a parting of the ways was inevitable.

The family breakup was painful, and the loss of our beloved island home made it doubly so for all of us - it created a deep sense of sadness and nostalgia that has stayed with me and my sisters to this day. Since those days though, we have all moved on with our busy lives. For me, revisiting our island home was too painful to contemplate - I felt, wrongly perhaps, that one should never go back, because many of those things that one held dear would inevitably have been changed. But life moves on, and little did I know that an opportunity that I could not possibly ignore would eventually present itself - albeit some sixty five years after my family had sold our wonderful island home.

An opportunity presents itself

And so it was, on a day in April 2015, that my sister Valerie telephoned to say that our 84 year old elder sister June was to be awarded her Honours degree at Swansea University in July. My wife Christine and I decided that we just had to be there to support her on the big day, and thus it was that the idea of combining a family celebration of her great achievement with a family visit to our beloved Skomer began to take shape. It was a perfect opportunity for my children and grandchildren to see that wonderful place where my sisters and I had grown up.

I contacted Rob Pickford, Chairman of the trustees of the Wildlife Trust of South and West Wales (WTSWW), the guardians of Skomer Island on behalf of Natural Resources Wales, to ask if a private family visit to Skomer could be arranged. This would not only be a nostalgic and emotional visit down memory lane, but would also be a great opportunity to be reassured that our much loved island home is now being cared for and protected in a manner that enables many to enjoy what we took for granted.

Rob and the WTSWW management and staff were kindness itself, and organised a private boat trip across to Skomer, together with personal attention to our needs at every stage of our visit. In spite of very uncertain weather conditions leading up to the day of our visit, the day itself dawned bright and sunny. It turned out to be an absolutely fabulous day throughout - such a happy coincidence of perfect conditions and moving memories.

What follows here is the story of that visit, with a series of pictures and reminiscences on what life on Skomer was really like for the last family to farm it.

A Marloes fisherman - about to make a withie lobster pot using a special stand

The start of a memorable day

On our way to the boat at Martins Haven - John Reynolds' 'Dale Princess' - we had to pass through Marloes village which was our first trigger of childhood memories. After stopping briefly to visit my grandparents' grave near the church gate, it soon became very evident that this village was no longer the working village that had been a part of our childhood – it was now a gentrified destination for holidaymakers. It seemed that the heart and soul of the old community that we knew so well had clearly gone for ever.

Marloes village used to be home to the fishermen who kept their boats at Martins Haven, and to local farming families and their agricultural workers. In our day it had a Post Office with a shop in the village square, run by Affie and Peggy Johns who also sold hardware on the other side of the road. I well remember the wonderment in 1948 when they installed a petrol pump – which in those days was operated manually using a long pump handle on the side of the cabinet.

Further up the village on the left there was also Emma's little shop, which sold some tinned food and cigarettes, etc.. Emma was always in a wheel chair and it was unusual for us to pass by on foot without dropping in for a chat. On the other side of the road, just before Emma's shop, lived Jack Edwards a local fisherman. Jack was a great help to my family when they were dealing with the early challenges of building a new life on Skomer. But more on Jack later.

Continuing on our journey from Marloes to Martins Haven we passed 'Treehill' and 'East Hook' farms - both of which in my youth had been occupied by my uncles and aunts and their families - and eventually reached Martins Haven car park. The car park takes up a corner of what used to be our cultivated field at the back of our mainland home, Martins Haven Cottage (now called Rath Cottage).

Martins Haven Cottage - our mainland home during the war years

During the WW2 years we had temporarily moved out from Skomer to live in this cottage. Although we still spent much time on the island, Martins Haven and the Deer Park was our home stamping ground over that period, and this part of our lives also has many memories for me and my sisters. Life on the mainland was naturally easier in many ways - we grazed animals on the Deer Park, grew some crops nearby, and Father was in charge of the Coastguard Station at Wooltack Point up on the Deer Park.

The island was a sanctuary from everyday wartime life over that period, but evidence of the war was everywhere on the mainland, even in this remote part of the country. On the eastern boundary of Martins Haven cottage, for example, there was the end of a decoy airfield runway. This was intended to attract the attention of the German bombers from the real airfield at Dale, from which a 'Free Polish Squadron' of Wellington bombers operated. Fortunately for us, the German bombers ignored it on their many sorties to blitz Swansea, and I can still vividly remember the red glow from that burning city lighting up the sky at night after each bombing raid.

And only a few hundred yards in the other direction, above Martins Haven cove and not far from Ronald Lockley's bungalow (now called Lockley Lodge) was an army searchlight battery and anti-aircraft gun emplacement. Hard to imagine today.

A growing sense
of anticipation

After an enthusiastic welcome by WTSWW staff we walked down towards Martins Haven beach, passing our old garages, now Public Conveniences. In our day these garages had also served as a workshop for the servicing of our outboard engines, and other such jobs. Lobster pots, using withies pulled from the Deer Park stream nearby, were also made there.

Many Marloes fishing boats operated out of Martins Haven in the 1940s and 50s

We arrived at the top of the beach approach and it was sad to see that the many fishing boats that used to cram the beach were no longer there. Nor were there any of the lobster pots awaiting their owners' attention, or the lobster storage chests that used to float just off the shore. Another way of life now long gone.

Unlike the wonderful weather of that day, Martins Haven beach could be particularly exposed when the winds were

Father leaving Skomer North Haven - note the ever present spare engine

northerly. During such times the journey to Skomer could be extremely hazardous, if not impossible. On one occasion, when the family had just returned from the usual weekly shopping trip to Haverfordwest, we found one of our boats being washed off the beach in an unexpectedly fierce winter's gale. I still vividly remember how a really vicious undertow of pebbles grabbed at my ankles and almost completely swept me away as we struggled to save the boat. It was only after a considerable struggle that we eventually managed to save it. Such experiences are of course all a part of a working island life.

Whilst waiting for the Skomer boat on that July day, other memories flooded in. I remember helping my father with various boat maintenance jobs on that beach; one such occasion was when several boat timbers needed to be replaced, and the new timbers had to be thoroughly steamed before they could be fitted. Island life develops self-reliance and ingenious extemporisation, and it was certainly so in this case.

Father found a piece of old iron pipe, bunged a large piece of cork in the end, put some water in the bottom, leaned it up against a rock at an angle, and lit a fire under it. In this way the timber inserted into the pipe steamed thoroughly, thereby allowing perfect shaping to the curve of the boat's planking. I particularly remember this occasion because the pipe slipped off the rock and hit me on the head, throwing me to the ground. (My wife Christine says that that explains a lot!)

There were many other memories of this beach, of those summer days when we would take dozens of nature lovers of all ages across to Skomer in our open boats, which were propelled by a small outboard engine. A spare engine was always carried in case of any unexpected mishap (such as losing an engine off the stern of the boat, which did happen on at least one occasion).

On really calm days the surface of the water would be as smooth as glass, and one could clearly discern the myriad of life on the seabed - an absolute delight. And sometimes, as evening was closing in, we would take friends out in the boat to fish close under the cliffs. The prize would be a good catch of a dozen pollock and mackerel for our supper.

Waiting on today's walkway at Martins Haven to embark on the Dale Princess

And so to the Island at last

The journey to Skomer today is very different indeed. There is now a walkway, built out over the rock promontory on the left side of Martins Haven bay, which ends at a point where the Dale Princess can safely embark passengers for the island. It works well, and one couldn't help thinking how much easier it was doing it this way – although one still couldn't help missing that closer exposure to the elements that was always a part of our much smaller open boat experience!

We duly set off for Skomer and, as we passed Wooltack Point, we could see the strong tide flow heading west. Anyone familiar with the Jack Sound tide race could not fail to anticipate a rough passage through the Sound if it was travelling North – but fortunately for us today the nearly top-of-the-tide westerly

A strong tide going west today as we passed Little Sound on our way to Skomer

The wreck of the SS Lonsdale which had been en-route from Belfast to Milfold Haven

direction meant that it was relatively calm on this occasion. Sadly, though, we did not see any sign of the porpoises that often escorted us on our passage through the sound.

I particularly remember one occasion when, with a boat full of visitors, someone spotted a little black blob on the horizon. It seemed to be headed for Ireland in the strong westerly tide, so we thought that perhaps we should investigate. Eventually, and much to our surprise, we saw that it was a man in swimming trunks, in what appeared to be a giant tyre inner tube. It turned out to be an airman from the nearby base at Dale, who had gone to sleep and floated out to sea in an aircraft inner tube. He was too frightened by the tide race to leave the tube and was saying his last prayers when we spotted him. I don't know which he found the worst - his frightening experience, or the fact that the Camp Commander was on our boat at the time!

There was a less welcome encounter in the Jack Sound during the wartime years, when one of our passengers spotted something on the horizon which eventually became recognisable as a mine that had obviously broken loose from its underwater moorings. As it floated past in the strong current, only a few yards from our boat, one could clearly see the long spikes that housed the detonators - it was a very sinister and eerie feeling to be only yards away from that menacing object bobbing about in the tide race. It was of course reported soon afterwards so that it could be detonated by rifle fire.

As we passed Midland island today it was not difficult to identify the spot where the SS Lonsdale had foundered in a ferocious gale in September 1938 (as did the SS Mosely on almost the same spot some years before). On that occasion in 1938, our father, mother and grandfather had braved the gale to rescue the crew of the Lonsdale. The fame that came to Mother in the national press was astonishing, with the press christening her Grace Darling the Second, because this rescue occurred exactly 100 years to the day of the original Grace Darling rescue.

And so we approached Skomer North Haven, and those vivid memories kicked in again. If we had been but two months earlier we would have been met by a cloud of bluebell perfume wafting down over the water, and puffins all around us, in the air and on the water – over 10,000 puffins can be found on Skomer during the breeding season. While it was a little sad that we had missed that experience, we were none the less delighted that there were still quite a few puffins swimming around. They must however always keep a weather eye open for any sly predatory greater black back

Mother, Grandfather and Father - after checking the shipwreck
serveral days after the storm had passed

Our arrival in North Haven today – still some puffins on the water to welcome us

gull swimming nearby which, if the slightest opportunity arose, would grab a puffin to make it release its catch.

As we came closer, we could now discern a steep railed path up the cliff from the disembarkation point. Undoubtedly this was an easier way of disembarking than that of old, but I couldn't help missing that exciting feeling when the keel of our open boat ran up the shingle and we leapt out to help the visitors to disembark. This new path up the cliff eventually joined the original track at its first hairpin bend, and it was here that we were made very welcome by the WTSWW resident wardens and volunteers. After a short briefing on their role in protecting the integrity of the island, and in supporting appropriate research, we briskly set off up the path.

Full of anticipation as we head for shore

Arriving on Skomer with visitors in 1949 - Mother poised to leap on shore

20

A trio of puffins - just observing life

Gull and chicks in nest - a commonplace Skomer sight

Memories of Island life
come flooding in

In the days when we farmed Skomer we had three main modes of transport, apart from shanks' pony of course. We had a pony called Billy, who had been on the island for many years after being taken there in the boat by my grandfather. We also had a Shire horse called Prince, a truly majestic animal, who was mainly used for pulling a sled dray between the North Haven beach and the farm house. He was also used to plough the first furrows - using a deep Wilmot plough - when bringing the fields back to cultivation, and for drilling furrows when planting early potatoes.

Getting Prince over to Skomer set us a major challenge, but eventually the decision was made to swim him across by the side of the boat. That worked very well for the first part of the journey, but

Heavily laden dray on its way to the North Haven Beach

Our Fordson tractor - had to be split into its parts to be able to transport in a small open boat

inevitably he tired, stopped swimming, and rolled over to have a rest. This acted like a drag anchor on the boat! Suffice it to say that, after several very sticky and hair-raising moments en-route, Prince strode heroically out of the water on to the North Haven beach. When we sold Skomer, we left Prince and Billy to end their days peacefully on the island.

Our third mode of island transport was a Fordson tractor. It was mainly used for the various cultivation tasks after the initial ploughing, and for powering a large circular saw for sawing large timbers that were often washed ashore after gales. Transporting this tractor to the island in our open boat was yet another major challenge. However, this was overcome by the construction of a tripod hoist on Martins Haven beach, which enabled us to hoist the tractor in separate parts and lower them into the boat which then floated when the tide came in. At the other end, the tractor had to be reassembled on North Haven beach before being driven up the path. Timing and tide were both critical to the success of this enterprise, of course.

As we walked up the path from North Haven, with the vivid memory of our Prince with his dray in my and my sisters' minds, we passed one of the old lime kilns that I had often explored as a boy. In days long gone the coastal barges would bring in limestone, which was burned and slaked in the lime kilns to produce fertiliser for the fields, and was also used in the mortar used in building. In our day we did not use those kilns, and any fertilisers that we needed had to be laboriously brought in to the island in 1 Cwt sacks, after their delivery to Martins Haven beachhead.

As we continued up the path towards the farm we noticed that there seemed to be much more bracken around than in our time. Noticeable also was the fact that there were far fewer shearwater carcases on the path, although we weren't sure why. The Manx Shearwater is very much a Skomer presence, and particularly noisy at night. They are birds of huge stamina – I remember that in 1938 a shearwater was ringed on Skomer and was caught again only ten days later in South America.

The Harold Stone - of uncertain origin

Ancient habitation in Skomer North Valley

At the top of the path, before we entered the first field, we stopped at Bread Rock and I reminded everyone that life on an island can be very different from the idyllic conditions of that day. We had lived on the island over many summers and winters, come rain or shine, storm or calm, and each had its own particular challenges and rewards. Even the challenge of really rough and alarming storms can be very exhilarating as the seas pound the cliffs, raising clouds of spume, and a wind so strong that it literally almost sweeps one off one's feet.

As for the rewards, they often came from the flotsam and jetsam, which provided surprisingly useful items for we island dwellers used to having to make-do. During the war I well remember grey cube-shaped life rafts, which had been washed off ships, coming ashore. They often contained tins of Pemmican and chocolate slabs, as well as tins of water - a veritable treasure trove for the island dweller. But enough of that while we stand in the sun reminiscing on this day in July 2016.

I harked back to an occasion in the winter of 1948, when a gale had sprung up, preventing contact with the mainland. We were all in the house, where Mother and Annie – our home help of many years – were cooking our evening meal, when my sister June hit her head violently while dashing through a passage under the stairs. Worryingly she developed severe muscle spasms, and it was clear that a doctor was needed. But how to arrange that in the prevailing conditions, with no radio communications of any kind and in the midst of a howling gale?

We knew that, in times of dire need, a distress fire should be lit on Bread Rock, but we had never before needed to put it to the test. However, it was certainly worth a try, so Father and Arnold - our elderly rabbit catcher – set off for Bread Rock with sufficient fuel to make a large fire, and a torch with which to flash distress signals. In the gale force wind it wasn't too difficult for them to get a raging fire going, which was soon seen by the coastguard on Wooltack Point. They also flashed the word 'doctor' in morse code, but unfortunately the coastguard's skill at reading morse was about as rudimentary as those sending the message, and he alerted the St. Davids lifeboat without mentioning the need for medical help.

The lifeboat arrived within the hour, but was in great danger of approaching too close to the rocky shore. To prevent any possibility of harm to the lifeboat in those turbulent conditions, Father

Prince and Billy drilling for potatoes - Father in charge - me helping

struggled out to it in our small boat to explain the situation. The crew radioed to Milford Haven for a doctor to come, and arranged for him to be collected from Martins Haven. He eventually arrived on Skomer some hours later, to find that June's symptoms were thankfully subsiding satisfactorily. How very different it is today, with mobile phones and Air/Sea rescue helicopters.

Turbulent seas battering Skomer's cliffs

Taking the lazy way to the North Haven - Grandfather with Billy pulling the dray

Haymaking - with family and school friends

28

Peregrine on our front lawn - being nursed back to health after an injury to its wing

A Peregrine with its well developed chick

Shearwater and chick in exposed nest

Kittiwakes on the ledges at The Wick

Guillmots nesting on ledges near the South Haven

And so to the family home

Our party then moved on from Bread Rock, and across two fields towards the ruins of our old home in the centre of the island. When Grandfather had bought the island he extensively modernised the farmhouse. He installed electricity, which was supplied by a Lister generator through a bank of commercial vehicle batteries, and a domestic water supply which was pumped from a spring near the North Pond. He had a first floor veranda built along the full length of the south facing front of the house, and also brought his beloved billiard table which he installed in the East Wing.

What for us, in those days, was a very comfortable family home, is now a sad ruin. As we entered the gates in front of the house it became only too clear how, over the years, the winter storms

Storms and neglect after our departure in 1950 soon ravaged our old home

Our dining Room in 1949 - ready for our ornithologist guests

have ravaged our lovely old home, leaving only the walls standing; although it still retains a certain charm under its ivy cladding. The WTSWW staff have rejuvenated the lawn in front of the house – indeed it looked rather better than in the days when we had a tennis court there! Some of the barns have also been restored to provide useful accommodation and facilities for visitors.

We went into what used to be our old dining room, now open to the sky. There were a number of helpful displays providing some historical facts about the island and its inhabitants, including our family of course. Behind the dining room lies our old kitchen, and my most vivid memory of that room was an occasion during WW2 when we called into the house on one of our many checks on the island. On the kitchen table was a saucer containing a bar of soap, which was still wet and which had obviously been used in the past few minutes. Clearly we had disturbed someone, most probably a German submariner (some days earlier Mother had spotted a submarine sheltering on the surface near the north shore). We returned hurriedly to the mainland to call the police, who eventually arrived fully armed, but no one was found and the mystery remained.

Today we all wandered around the house surrounds, noting the ancient bacon curing ovens set into the north side of the house next to our old billiards room. We never used those ovens, although we had bred pigs, but we cured our bacon in brine. On an island one has to be pretty self-sufficient and, in addition to the pigs, we kept cows for milk and for making butter, chickens and geese for eggs and the table, and sheep for their fleeces. And of course rabbits were in very plentiful supply all over the island; an eclectic mix of colours and types – white, black, angora as well as the usual grey.

Indeed, the sale of rabbits was a useful addition to our income, as was the sale of early daffodils that grew in profusion in beds along the front of the house. Gulls' eggs were also in great demand by the best hotels in London, and we would send quantities via the Great Western Railway from Haverfordwest. When collecting the eggs we were careful only to collect from nests where there was just one egg – any more would indicate the possibility of at least one being addled. We were never too sensitive about collecting the eggs of the greater black back gulls - they were possibly the fiercest predators on the island, as evidenced by the many hundreds of shearwater corpses that littered the paths.

Our family home on Skomer in 1948 with Val going for a ride on Billy

June doing the milking - no machines in those days

Our breeding livestock included beef cattle, which were mostly Herefords, and Kerry Hill and Suffolk sheep, flocks of which were confined to grazing on The Neck. The shepherding of these could be an extremely hazardous task, with sheep looking for good grazing frequently having to be rescued by Father from the ledges and gullies on the cliff edge - at considerable risk to life and limb!

On our visit to the house it was most surprising to find the little wooden bungalow on the east side of the converted barn still fully intact. During the war years, Father and I used to stay overnight in that bungalow when visiting the island on rabbit hunting trips. Our stay was never likely to be a restful experience, because of the continuous cacophony from the shearwaters nesting underneath the bungalow floor. But it was always a worthwhile experience, and our evening meal of winkles, picked off the rocks in North Haven on our way up, was an enjoyable repast at the end of a long day.

Our rabbiting dog 'team' consisted of Tina, a lurcher who was very fast at catching the rabbits dazzled in the torch beam, and Trudie a spaniel who would retrieve them from Tina and carry them back to us. They worked together as a well drilled team and, once a sack was full, Father would hide it under the nearest rock outcrop, to be collected, with the many other sacks, in the early morning.

Today, after looking at the site of the old horse roundabout at the back of the South Barn, used in the very old days to turn the corn grinding stone inside the barn, we retired to the high rock behind the yard. We relaxed over a nice picnic lunch, reflecting on what an enjoyable morning it had been. Sadly time was not really on our side though, so we decided that a walk to The Wick, to see the kittiwakes and some remaining puffins on the opposite bank, would be the wisest course.

We followed the well-marked path to The Wick, and dallied for a while to enjoy the bird life on the ledges and banks. The view down The Wick inlet was quite dramatic, and some family members managed to get very close to the puffins, much to the excitement of the grandchildren. We then followed the path back to the North Haven, and being somewhat early for our return boat, went down the path to the beach to relax while we waited.

I was always slightly nervous of our geese

Sheep on The Neck - going to the sheep pen to be checked for fly blow and maggots

Sheep shearing - with June providing the power

Father rabbiting - a centuries old Skomer tradition

Our wartime overnight base - not a quiet night with the underfloor shearwater chorus

Valerie and me, with Trudie and Tina - our constant companions

1946 help - Back row: Cousin Brindley, Joseph Koch (German POW), Artie (handyman) and
Front row: Father, Mother and me

June was always ready to take on an orphan

Regards from June Codd.

Some final recollections

My very first thought when we reached the beach was to look for my name on the concrete winch base; I had idly marked it in the concrete when Father and I had constructed the base all those years ago. I was only just able to discern it in the front right hand corner, although I am sure that no one else would recognise it. That was quite an emotional moment for me.

And as we looked out across the North Haven at a lone sailing boat lying at anchor, I was reminded of the French fishing boats that occasionally visited the North Haven to seek shelter when weather conditions from a southerly direction were threatening. We would take Annie Lloyd, our Welsh speaking housekeeper, out to the French boat. It appeared that the Welsh and Breton

Skomer North Haven - the 'gateway' to the Island

Bedding down calves, on their way to Skomer for fattening

languages were so similar that each could understand the other, enabling her to indulge in a spot of bartering - some freshly caught rabbits for lobsters and langoustine. This was a culinary treat for we island dwellers, particularly when we had so little time to set our own lobster pots. Dear Annie. We all loved her dearly.

On this day in July I reflected on the fact that this beach had always been the sole landing point for the island, and was therefore the main channel through which absolutely everything flowed. As such, it held many memories for me. There was always a deep sense of anticipation whenever I was going to the mainland on an errand, or returning after a rough crossing and looking forward to getting back home; but most of all I was reminded of the incredibly difficult challenges and tribulations associated with this place.

Just stop and reflect for a moment. If you order a ton of coal on the mainland, it is delivered by lorry to your home coal bunker. For Skomer it was delivered to the top of the approach to Martins Haven beach. Twenty 1 cwt bags of coal would then have to be carried on our backs, down the beach to our boat, and across the water to the North Haven beach, where they would be lifted out of the boat and carried up the beach to the quayside. The twenty 1cwt

Positioning over 13cwt of beef for the return journey

bags would then be loaded on to the dray, to be pulled by Prince for nearly a mile inland to the house, where we could finally unload it into our coal bunker - just one example of the huge amount of extra time and effort that was called for in everyday life on the island.

That same hard slog applied to every item of the big weekly shop in Haverfordwest, and to the constant stream of needs for the farm. And if we had a special building project, which was not unusual, it would pose its own transport challenges. At one point an ex-military amphibious DUKW landing craft had to be used to transport very cumbersome and heavy building materials to the island.

But perhaps the most dramatic challenge on that beach was when very large fattened cattle had to be taken to the mainland for sale. The verdant pastures of Skomer always produced the very topmost grade of animal, beasts so large that there was always a danger of them holing the bottom of the boat. This challenge called for special measures to be taken, the first of which was to bring over to the island several strong men from Marloes village.

Four strong men, two planks and one good heave does the trick

And quickly roped down in the soft fern bedding

The targeted animal had to be corralled up against the side of the specially modified open boat that we used for this purpose. Two of those men would then slide strong planks under the beast's belly, resting one end of the planks on the side of the boat. A well timed heave would pitch the animal into the prepared fern bed in the bottom of the boat, where it would quickly be roped down so that it could not cause harm to itself or the boat. Compared to the cattle, the transportation of sheep was a doddle, but it still imposed an additional task that mainland farmers did not have to contend with.

Father told me the story about how on one occasion, after the boat had been beached overnight on the mainland, a rat had leapt out from the fern bedding in the bottom of the boat upon its arrival back at Skomer North Haven. Fortunately diligent trapping over the following days caught the rat which was found to be about to produce young. A threat to Skomer's vermin-free state was thus narrowly avoided.

Some of the unhappiest memories that this beach evoked for me were those of my return to boarding school at the start of each term. I simply hated the very thought of going away, and was always overjoyed when we were stormbound for a week or two at the start of a new term. Living on the island did of course mean that boarding school for me and my sisters from the tender age of six years old could not be avoided.

It was an especially sad time also when Grandfather, who in his later years lived in Dover, had cancer and returned to his beloved Skomer to die. He was very weak and in a great deal of pain, but was determined to spend his last days on the island that he loved so dearly. I can so understand how he felt, because this unique place does cast a spell that one never really shakes off. He now lies in Marloes churchyard with Grandmother.

And then there were the happier memories; the joy of returning after a long absence, the wonderment of the raucous bird life all around, watching the seals rearing their young on the beaches. And yet at times one could still find complete tranquillity in all that frenzy, and be in another world entirely. What powerful, and often conflicting, memories.

And finally leaving the boat at Martins Haven - ready for road transport

A docile cow enjoying the trip - a happy passenger under a comforting hand!

Sheep were a far easier proposition

Two seals enjoying the surf

Seal Pup suckling - on North Haven Beach

'Mummy - Where are you?'

A sad departure

And so, after such a wonderful day, we went back up the path to thank our kind hosts, and to embark for the return journey to Martins Haven. The water was relatively calm and the journey uneventful – in contrast to many crossings that I remembered from the past, particularly those in the winter months when the conditions were most challenging.

The strength of the wind and of the tide, and how the two interact with each other, are undoubtedly one of the biggest challenges to be faced in island life. However, when both of those are least in evidence, dense fog could make the journey even more nerve-wracking. Father always kept an old ship's compass handy (it came off the Lonsdale I think) for those occasions when fog was likely. In such challenging conditions we knew that our journey home would be really difficult, with a visibility of no more than ten yards in the dense swirling mists and the fog horns on St Anne's Head playing tricks on one's sense of direction.

During the war years there were many winter trips to the island when I was really glad to be safely back in the warm in Martins Haven Cottage - such as after a couple of days of catching rabbits on Skomer. On our way back from the island I would often be huddled in the stern of the boat, with breaking waves on our quarter, and concentrating on steering while trying to avoid the freezing driving spray. Meanwhile Father would be sitting amidships gutting the rabbits and throwing the paunches into the sea.

Upon our arrival at Martins Haven we would carry about 200 gutted rabbits up to our garage to hang overnight, ready for Tommy Reynolds from Marloes to collect for market on the following day (Tommy would carry virtually anything in his large old Austin saloon - 200 rabbits one day, and the bride to her wedding the next!).

Father used to say that the sea is a good servant but a bad master, and he was so right. At the start of this foray through my memories, I mentioned Jack Edwards who lived in Marloes. Jack was a quiet unassuming man, and a highly competent seafarer in whom all could place complete trust. As such he was a great help to Grandfather during his early years on Skomer. In fact Grandfather owed his life to Jack.

On this memorable occasion, Grandfather needed to take supplies, including coal, to the island and was accompanied by Jack, who was always ready to help. They set off from Martins Haven but the weather conditions rapidly deteriorated soon after leaving. After battling against an ever increasing head-wind they eventually had to abort the attempt, but by this time had lost any opportunity to make landfall again at Martins Haven. As darkness fell, and the storm continued unabated, they could only run with the wind, their sail in complete tatters, hoping against hope to find shelter.

In the stormy darkness they eventually found themselves passing the Stack Rock in the south east corner of St. Brides Bay. This was their very last opportunity to find shelter, and they only just managed to row in under the lea of the Stack Rock. Holding that position in such turbulent conditions was well-nigh impossible, so they threw a sack of coal, tied to a line, over the side in the hope that it would act as a drag anchor. Unfortunately, after a short time, the sack broke open on the sea bed, and had to be replaced by the second – and last – bag. This bag eventually suffered the same fate, and the two totally exhausted men could only try and maintain their position as best they could in the turbulent waters under the lea of the Stack Rock.

Meanwhile, the emergency services had been out all night scouring the coastline, and Father and Mother had virtually given up all hope of ever seeing Grandfather alive again. It was not until the following morning, when the worst of the storm had largely abated, that someone in Little Haven village thought that they could see a boat out near the Stack Rock. Both totally exhausted men were safely brought ashore, and so another small, but not untypical, episode in Skomer's history ended happily.

And so to the end
of a wonderful day

After we had disembarked at Martins Haven on that lovely July day, with so many memories and emotions still welling up inside me, what were my feelings as I reflected on the wonderful day? I realised of course that at the centre of island life as we remembered it, were our father and mother, Reuben and Betty Codd. They are no longer with us, but this story is really theirs, not ours.

Their story was about two young people from completely different backgrounds, who found themselves in this wonderful but extremely challenging place. Those backgrounds naturally engendered different personal priorities and expectations of life, which were hard to reconcile. But in the early years their love of this island, and their deep sense of personal responsibility for safeguarding and nurturing such a unique place, provided the common bond and shared tenacity of purpose needed to farm on Skomer and bring up a family on this remote island.

Farming is a tough enough life at the best of times, but on a remote island it poses huge additional challenges, and the realities of island life were such that one was seldom able to stop for a moment to enjoy the sheer magic of life in such a place. Time for occasional relaxation, such as a game of tennis or a swim in the South Haven, was indeed a rare luxury.

The reality of island life was the constant backlog of urgent tasks, most of which needed someone highly competent in a wide range of practical skills. Those essential skills encompassed blacksmithing, joinery, animal husbandry which included shoeing the horses, building construction, catering for visitors and providing facilities for research projects, as well as dealing with all manner of emergencies. The routine replenishment of essentials from the mainland also filled a great deal of one's time. And so it went on......................

The Codd family thrived for many years on that hard, but very satisfying existence, but the never ending pressures to survive commercially, together with the constant challenges of island life, eventually proved too much for one family to cope with on their own. The disruption of the wartime years had also played its part in undermining family cohesiveness, hence the sale of the island in 1950, and the end of an era in Skomer's farming history.

And what was the most important conclusion that we took away from our family's return trip to Skomer in July 2015? – It was that we should rest assured that the Wildlife Trust of South and West Wales is proving to be a worthy guardian of this unique place, the place that the Codd family did their very best to protect and nurture over so many years, and the place which now forms a wonderful heritage for all to enjoy in perpetuity.

Our family group visiting Skomer in July 2015. Sadly our son Justin
and his family were unable to join us that day

Back row: (left to right) Me, my wife Christine, Valerie, Tom (June's Partner) and June
Middle row: Daughters Louise and Emma and son-in-law Noel
Front row: Grandchildren Emily, Daniel and Izzy